MEASURING UP

weight

Peter Patilla

Belitha Press

First published in the UK in 1999 by

Belitha Press Limited
London House, Great Eastern Wharf
Parkgate Road, London SW11 4NQ

This edition first published in 2000

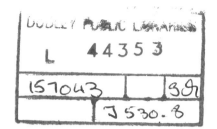

Editor: Claire Edwards
Designer: Simeen Karim
Picture researcher: Diana Morris
Consultant: Martin Hollins

Thanks to Graham Peacock, Sheffield Hallam University,
for his help with some of the science ideas.

ISBN 1 84138 155 1 (paperback)
ISBN 1 85561 887 7 (hardback)

Printed in Singapore

British Library Cataloguing in Publication Data
for this book is available from the British Library.

Picture acknowledgements:
AKG London: 13b. **Avery Berkel:** 19t. **BIPM:** 13t. **Bridgeman
Art Library:** 8c Private Collection. **British Museum:** 4b ET Archive.
C M Dixon: front cover l, 6, 7t. Mary Evans PL: 15b, 18b. **Eye
Ubiquitous:** 20 Yiorgos Nikiteas. **Werner Forman:** 5c Private
Collection. **Getty Images:** back cover & 21 World Perspectives,
29t Joern Rynio. Powerstock/Zefa: 22, 23 Charles Tyler, 25b, 28b,
29b Andy Rouse. **Science & Society PL:** front cover br, 8t, 17b.
Spectrum CL: front cover tr, 15t, 19b, 26, 27t. **Stockmarket:** 11b.

CONTENTS

Mass and weight

In everyday speech the word *weight* means an object used to measure how heavy things are. It can also mean how heavy something feels. Scientists make a distinction between weight and mass, which is explained on pages 20 and 21.

IN THE BEGINNING

All through history people have needed to weigh things such as food, medicines and precious metals. The first weights were based on what a man or animal could hold, carry or haul.

People began comparing weights by holding an object in each hand and deciding whether one was heavier, or if they weighed about the same. Many years passed before someone had the brain wave of making a balance by tying a cord round the centre of a stick. The items to be compared were tied on to the stick, one at each end. If they were the same weight the stick remained level. If one object was heavier then the stick tilted.

Weighty Fact
The first weights were made from everyday materials, including the ripe seeds of plants such as liquorice and carob. By 3000 BC the Egyptians were using stones as weights.

First weights

As the years passed ancient civilizations developed standard weights for everyday needs, such as buying and selling. The Babylonians and Egyptians made their weights into much more interesting shapes than the plain lumps of metal we use today. They crafted them into shapes to represent gods, animals and everyday objects. The first Babylonian weight was called the *mina*. Archaeologists have found *mina* weights shaped like ducks and swans.

Ancient Egyptians believed that when they died their heart would be weighed against a feather to see how truthful they had been in life. Paintings such as this one show the myth, but also tell us how Egyptians weighed things in everyday life.

Egyptian kites

From about 3000 BC the Egyptians used weights called *kites*. The weight of these changed over the years. Some were as light as 4.5 grams, others weighed as much as 29.9 grams. They were shaped like humans and animals, or moulded into beautiful geometric shapes.

Did you know?
The Ashanti people of West Africa used weights in the shape of crocodiles, cockroaches, birds and fish until the nineteenth century. People made up the correct weight by cutting off the heads, tails or legs.

An Ashanti weight shaped like an elephant. It was used for weighing gold dust.

Chinese weights

In 221 BC the Chinese Emperor, Shih Huang Ti, decided that his empire needed a standard unit of weight. He gave orders that the basic weight would be the *chih* (also called the *tan*). The *chih* was about 60 kilograms. During this time merchants developed a special way to double-check the weight of two very important products – grain and wine. The wine or grain was poured into a standard-sized vase. When the vase was struck, the sound varied according to how much was in it. This was surprisingly accurate.

INVADERS AND TRADERS

The weights used in one country were spread to others through trade and invasions.

Between about 1000 BC and 400 AD the most important traders, explorers and invaders were the Greeks followed by the Romans. The main Greek weight was called a *talent* and weighed 25.8 kilograms. The Romans adapted the Greek system using weights called *libra*.

Invaders

As the Romans conquered Europe, Western Asia and Africa their units of weight became the basis for many weighing systems around the world. Between the seventh and eleventh centuries they were adapted by other traders and invaders, such as the Vikings from Scandinavia and the Arabs from North Africa.

A Greek weight called a mina, weighing 470 grams. The Greeks adapted the Egyptian and Babylonian measuring systems, and sometimes used the same names.

Weighty Fact

Rulers tried to enforce standard weights to make it easier to collect taxes from people. Taxes were usually demanded as goods such as grain rather than money.

Weighty confusion

By the Middle Ages the Roman units of weighing were still used right across Europe. The trouble was that these units had changed over time and in different areas, not just from country to country, but even from city to city. Different countries tried to make their own laws saying which standard units of weight must be used. Even where this worked, when different countries traded with each other there was still some confusion.

An emperor's ruling

At the end of the eighth century an emperor called Charlemagne ruled many of the countries in Europe. He tried very hard to make all the traders in countries he ruled use the same measures. In 789 AD he introduced a weight called the *karlspfund*, which weighed 365 grams, but people carried on using weights they were used to.

Trade fairs

During the twelfth and thirteenth centuries there were trade fairs across Europe where people came to buy and sell all kinds of goods. The fairs made traders use the same weighing system wherever they came from. This helped the traders and many of them continued to use the system when they went home to their own country.

A Roman balance made from bronze. The weight is moved along the bar to balance any object fixed to the hook. This kind of balance is called a steelyard.

Explorers and settlers

From about 1565 many Europeans sailed to the United States of America and settled there. They took with them their systems of weighing and measuring, which then spread to the American colonies. The modern American weights are based on these early European measurements.

WEIGHING SYSTEMS

All weighing systems are made up of different units of weight used together. Several smaller units add up to one larger unit.

Ideally the units are figures that can be easily multiplied and divided to make bigger or smaller amounts. Standard units are the units that everyone agrees to use. For practical reasons there are different units for weighing different things. For instance, weighing a carrot in tonnes, or a car in grams would not be very sensible.

A standard weight used in Britain from about 1495 to 1601. This was a time when business was really booming.

This picture shows tea being weighed out in China, in the nineteenth century. Tea had to be weighed very carefully because it was an expensive, luxury item.

Troy weights

The French town of Troyes held very important markets and fairs during the Middle Ages. The system of weights and measures was carefully controlled, as at all fairs. Their system of weights became known as troy weights and was used to weigh precious metals and stones. There are 12 ounces in a troy pound.

Avoirdupois weights

At fairs less valuable items such as sugar or grain were measured using weights that were heavier than those used for precious metals. They were called avoirdupois weights. There are 16 ounces in an avoirdupois pound. Avoirdupois weights are the basis for the American and British weighing systems. They include tons and hundredweights.

Imperial weights

In 1824 the British parliament declared that all standard weights in Britain should be called imperial weights. These weights included the avoirdupois pound, which was introduced to Britain in the thirteenth century. A pound was divided into ounces, ounces into drams and drams into grains. A grain was the smallest unit of weight. It was based on a grain of wheat because this was the seed most commonly found across Europe. Grains are still used as units of weight today. There are 7000 grains in one pound weight.

Weighty Fact
The weight called a stone dates from when people used real stones as weights. The only stone still used is the British stone, which weighs 14 pounds.

Weights in America

When America became a united nation in 1783, its leaders realized how important it was to have a standard system of weights and measures. In 1821 The Secretary of State, John Quincy Adams, proposed that America should adopt the metric system of measurement, as France had. Congress did not agree, and the United States decided to continue with a slight adaptation of the British system of weights. The USA is the only large country still using weights such as pounds and ounces. They are called US customary weights.

People once used real stones to weigh things. Today the stone weight is usually used for weighing people.

POUNDS AND OUNCES

Which is heavier: a pound of gold or a pound of feathers?

Some people think the answer to this riddle is a pound of gold, because gold is heavier than feathers. Others say that the gold and feathers weigh the same because a pound weight has been used to compare them. The clever answer is that gold is weighed in troy pounds, which are different from the pounds we use for weighing everyday things. A troy pound is lighter than a standard pound, which makes a pound of feathers heavier than a pound of gold.

Did you know?
Many years ago in Britain there were six different weights all called a pound. Different pounds were used to weigh coins, gold, wool or everyday goods.

How weights change

A hundredweight is 112 pounds, which may seem strange. But the original hundredweight came from a rule made by Alfred the Great in the 800s. He defined a 'weight' as the weight of a container of water that was a handspan wide in all directions. A hundred of these made a hundredweight. King Edward I, who was King of England between 1272 and 1307, decided that a hundredweight should become 112 pounds. He made the change in two stages. First the hundredweight became 108 pounds so that people could become used to the idea!

Naming the pound

Have you ever wondered why some weights are called pounds, and why the word is shortened to lbs and not p or pd? The ancient Romans are to blame. The word pound comes from a Roman phrase *libra pondo*, which means 'one pound by weight'. Some cultures used the second word *pondo*, which means 'by weight', as a unit of weight. Over the years this became the word pound.

Where does lb come from?

Other cultures took the first word, *libra*, as the name of their measuring unit. The shortened form of *libra* is lbs. The shortened form was also used by the countries which used the word pound. It probably made trading easier between countries which had different words for the same weight.

How ounces came about

When measuring length the ancient Romans used their feet. To make sure a foot was always the same length they made copper bars. The length of the bars probably matched the foot size of one of the Roman emperors. The weight of a copper foot ruler became the weight of a pound. Each bar was divided into 12. The Roman for a twelfth part was *uncia*, and from this word ounce and inch developed. In Roman times there were 12 ounces to a pound, but over the next few hundred years this became 16 ounces.

Pounds and ounces are still used in many shops around the world, especially in the USA and Britain.

KILOGRAMS AND GRAMS

Metric weights are now the most common in the world. This is especially true in science and trade, where kilograms and grams are the international units of weight.

The metric system was introduced during the French Revolution, in the 1790s, by a committee of scientists and politicians. Instead of using measurements where there were 16 ounces in a pound, the new system used easy numbers such as tens, hundreds and thousands. This made long, complicated calculations much easier. The metric system used new weights called kilograms and grams. There are 1000 grams in a kilogram.

Napoleon Bonaparte

For all people, for all time

In 1799 French politicians launched the metric weighing system with the slogan 'For all people, for all time'. After the French Revolution, France was ruled by Napoleon Bonaparte. His armies conquered most of Europe and they took the metric system of weighing with them. Sometimes people resisted using metric measures as a political protest. Sometimes people just preferred the system they were used to. It has taken many years for metric weights to be used by everyone in Europe. In Britain people still use a mixture of metric and imperial weights.

Antoine Laurent Lavoisier

Antoine Lavoisier was born in France in 1743. He became a very clever scientist and spent many years helping to develop the metric system and working out how heavy a kilogram should be. He was guillotined during the French Revolution, five years before the metric system was officially adopted.

The kilogram

When the kilogram was first introduced scientists decided that the weight of water needed to fill a 10 centimetre cube would be called 1 kilogram. Because water was easily available this was used as the standard measurement. But then scientists decided that this was not accurate enough. They made a metal cylinder from platinum and iridium, which would not be affected by heat and cold, and used this as the standard weight instead. Today a special metal cylinder is used to check that all the kilograms used all over the world weigh exactly the same.

A cylinder of metal weighing 1 kilogram is kept under three glass domes in a vault in France at the International Bureau of Weights and Measures. Every kilogram must weigh exactly the same as this one. There are several copies of the kilogram weight in different parts of the world, including Washington DC, USA.

Weighty Fact
At first the kilogram was called a kilograve. The word grave meant heavy. It was soon changed to kilogram when the gram became a unit of weight.

Antoine Lavoisier (probably second from the left), working in his laboratory. The picture was painted in about 1785 by his wife (seated).

CHEATING THE WEIGHTS

All through history some people have tried to cheat others and clever people have worked hard to find ways of catching them out.

Archimedes was a Greek mathematician who was born in about 285 BC in Syracuse, Italy. The King of Syracuse thought that his new gold crown felt lighter than it should for its size, and wanted to know if the gold had been mixed with something else. He asked Archimedes to find out if he had been cheated. People say that while Archimedes was climbing into his bath, he noticed that the water level rose. This gave him an idea. He put the crown into a container of water, and a block of solid gold (the same weight as the crown was supposed to be) into a container with the same amount of water. He put the same weight of silver into a third container. The water rose higher for the crown and for the silver than for the gold, so Archimedes knew the king had been cheated.

Water rising around a solid object like this is called displacement. The bigger the object, the greater the displacement.

Coining it in

Originally coins were lumps of metal. They were worth as much as the weight of metal they were made from. This is why the names of some coins such as pound, *lira* and *drachma* are also units of weight. People used to cheat by chiselling bits off coins and clipping small pieces from the edges. They then sold the metal pieces or made new coins from them. During the seventeenth century a machine was invented that put grooves round the edge of coins, so people could see that they hadn't been touched. Today coins are worth the value stamped on them, not what they weigh.

This picture shows England's King Henry VII at a special trial in 1497, where unfair weights and measures were burnt.

Baker's dozen

A dozen means 12 of anything, but a baker's dozen means 13. This was because bread used to be sold by weight. It was such an important food that people didn't trust bakers to sell the right weight. Strict laws were passed in England in 1266 that led to bakers giving 13 loaves to the dozen, just in case any of them were underweight. Bakers were sent to the stocks if they baked loaves which weighed less than they should.

Did you know?
In New York, in 1906, many merchants cheated their customers. They hid weights inside food and bent the dials on their scales. A man called Patrick Derry sorted them out and the slogan 'honest weight' was invented.

Royal approval

In many places merchants used one set of weights for buying goods and another, lighter, set for selling. In 1357 King Edward III of England ordered that official weights and balances should be sent to every sheriff in the land to check that people used the same weights for buying and selling. But stopping people cheating remained a problem.

UNUSUAL WEIGHTS

Over the past thousand years weights and their names have changed. Nowadays most people use kilograms and grams, or pounds and ounces. But special weights are still used for some materials.

Valuable gem stones such as diamonds, rubies, emeralds and sapphires are weighed in carats. In the Middle Ages the carat was based upon the weight of grains of corn. Different countries used different amounts of grain. For hundreds of years people could not agree which carat to use. But in 1913 all countries agreed that a carat should weigh one fifth of a gram.

Did you know?
Women's stockings have denier numbers. A denier number gives the weight in grams of 9000 metres of fine materials, such as silk. So 15 denier stockings are made from yarn that weighs 15 grams for every 9000 metres.

Weights of long ago

Hundreds of years ago British weights had some wonderful and descriptive names. Cereals such as barley and oats were weighed in units called bushels, firlots, hobbets and windles. A bushel of barley was 50 pounds, but a bushel of oats was only 39 pounds. Fruit was weighed in barrels, sieves and cases. Butter was weighed in firkins, and cheese in cloves, stones and weys.

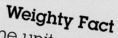

Weighty Fact
Some units of weight were named after their containers. Hobbets and windles were both kinds of basket used to carry seed or corn. Bushels and firkins were types of barrel.

These brass weights were used by an apothecary in the eighteenth century. The balance is about 100 millimetres tall.

Medicines and potions

In the past chemists were called apothecaries. When they needed to weigh medicines, potions and drugs, they used weights called grains, scruples, drams (also spelled drachm) and troy ounces. There were 20 grains in a scruple, 3 scruples in a dram and 8 drams in a troy ounce. To make things difficult, there are 16 drams in an avoirdupois ounce. Today drams are still used to describe a measure of drink.

Body weight

Body weight is important in many sports events. It would be unfair for a heavy person to wrestle with a light person. So in some sports, such as boxing, wrestling and weightlifting, men and women are grouped according to their weight. From the lightest to the heaviest these sports use names such as flyweight, bantamweight, lightweight, welterweight, middleweight and heavyweight.

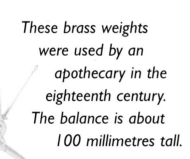

WEIGHING IN

Over the centuries people have used many different scales and balances to weigh things.

One of the earliest balances ever found dates back to the Ancient Egyptians in 5000 BC. Early balances had pans hanging from the ends by cords. The Romans improved the design by putting a pin through the centre as a balancing point. In the eighteenth century the centre pin was replaced by a knife edge. Knife edge balancing allowed accurate balancing instruments to be made. Today some balances still use pivots, but others are electronic or use quartz fibres.

In 1614 an Italian scientist called Santorio Santorio invented a weighing chair to test what happens to body weight after eating. He sat in the chair for 24 hours, and weighed all he ate and drank in that time.

Weighty Fact
Changes in the Earth's gravity can be measured using a gravimeter. This has a spring that lengthens or shortens according to the pull of gravity.

Heavy and light

Weighbridges are used to measure the weight of very heavy items. Lorries are driven on to weighbridges and weighed, to make sure that they are not overloaded. At the other extreme, microbalances use quartz fibres to weigh minute weights. The divisions on the reading scale can record weights as small as 0.0001 of a milligram. Microbalances are used in scientific research and in the chemical industry, where materials have to be weighed very accurately.

The sliding doors on this microbalance protect the small amount of powder being weighed from being blown away and from the effect of wind pressure on the balance.

Weighing food

Different balances are used depending on what is being weighed and how accurately. Supermarkets usually have electronic scales that give digital readouts. Some shops have pivot scales. These have weights on one side that can be changed to find how heavy the object is on the other side. Your food scales at home probably have a spring inside them that squashes down and shows the weight of the food on a dial.

Many market traders still use scales like the ones used by the Romans. Two pans hang from a bar that has a centre pin as a balancing point.

WEIGHT AND MASS

When your scales tell you how much you weigh, what they are really measuring is not your weight, but the amount of stuff your body is made of – which is called mass.

Weight and mass are different. Weight is the effect of gravity pulling on mass. The more gravity there is, the heavier something is. Astronauts on the Moon weigh less than on Earth, because there is less gravity there. But they have a mass that is the same on Earth as on the Moon. To be really accurate we should talk about the mass of an object rather than its weight.

When you throw a ball, it is pulled to the ground by gravity.

Gravity and force

The scientific unit of weight is called a newton, named after Sir Isaac Newton (1642–1727), one of the world's greatest scientists. People say that a falling apple gave Newton the idea of a force pulling things to Earth. The force of gravity on a mass of 1 kilogram is about 10 newtons. You can feel the force of about 1 newton by picking up an apple. When you stand on scales, they convert your weight in newtons into mass in kilograms.

More or less gravity

Gravity is the force that keeps the Earth moving round the Sun, and the Moon orbiting the Earth. All objects have some gravity pulling on them, even this book. Objects on the Earth weigh six times heavier than on the Moon.

Space weights

The same object weighs different amounts on different planets. If the mass of an astronaut is 80 kilograms, you can see below what he or she would weigh on different planets, measured in newtons. The density of a planet will also affect the astronaut's weight. The inner planets, Earth, Mercury, Mars and Venus, have more density than the outer planets.

Earth	**800N**
Pluto	**56N**
Mercury	**304N**
Mars	**304N**
Venus	**728N**
Uranus	**720N**
Saturn	**880N**
Neptune	**880N**
Jupiter	**2080N**

This astronaut may look weightless, but he is actually moving round the Earth at high speed. It is the same kind of weightlessness when someone free-falls without a parachute.

Density

People often assume that big objects will weigh more than small objects, but if you had the same weight of popcorn and pebbles you would have a much bigger pile of popcorn. This is because the density of pebbles is greater than that of popcorn. If you divide an object's mass by its size (volume) you find out its density.

Did you know?
If you weigh yourself at the South Pole and then weigh yourself on the Equator, you will be lighter on the Equator. This is because you are nearer the centre of the Earth at the poles.

FORCES AND WEIGHT

We use the word force in many ways. In science it has a special meaning. It is a push or a pull.

You use a force to move a bicycle or to lift a book. There are different kinds of forces. As well as the force produced by gravity, there is the sticking force of friction and the upthrust force of water that means we can float.

The force of wind resistance can be used to slow down falling weights – even human beings.

Did you know?
A famous scientist called Galileo dropped two cannon balls weighing different amounts from the top of Pisa tower, in Italy. He found that they landed at the same time.

Equal forces
If you hang a stone from a spring, gravity pulls it down and the air pushes up against it. If you put the stone into water it seems to weigh less, because the water is pushing up with a stronger force than air. You can feel the force of water when you try to push a cork under water and hold it there.

A balancing act

When forces balance, things don't move. When forces are not balanced, movement changes, so a bicycle goes faster, or a ball drops to the ground. Counterweights are weights used to balance heavy objects to stop them toppling over. The weight of a counterbalance has to be worked out very carefully so that the forces are balanced.

Forces and transport

A ship that has a mass of 500 000 tonnes pushes down into the sea with a force of 5 000 000 000 (5 billion) newtons. The sea pushes up with a force of 5 000 000 000 (5 billion) newtons. The force of the sea is the same as the weight of the ship, so the ship floats. Because scientists and engineers know how to work out weights and forces, they can design aeroplanes that stay up in the sky and ships that float.

Heavy blocks are put on the short arm of cranes to stop the long arm tipping the crane over.

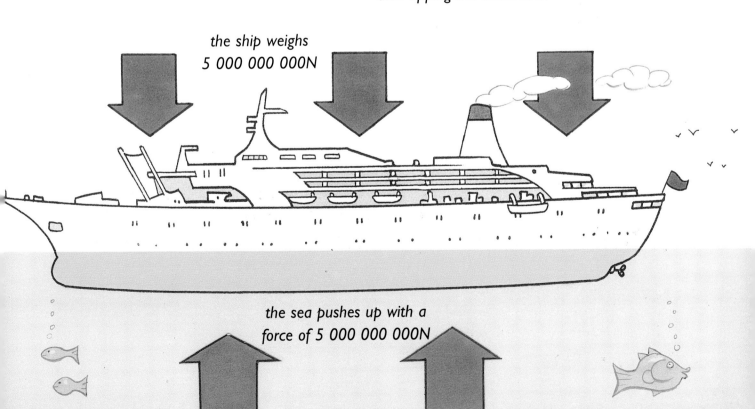

the ship weighs 5 000 000 000N

the sea pushes up with a force of 5 000 000 000N

NOT FOR WEIGHING

Weights have been used in many ways through the ages – not just for weighing.

Ancient Egyptian builders used small weights hung on lengths of string to check whether something was vertical. The string was tied to an F-shaped frame. When a builder placed the frame against a wall, he could see whether the wall was perfectly upright or if it was sloping. The tool was forgotten about for many years, but was rediscovered later. The weight at the end of the line is called a plumb bob.

Weighty Fact
If a racehorse runs very well in several races it may have weights placed in its saddle to slow it down. This is called a handicap, and gives other horses a chance to win a race.

Weight belts

When people go diving they put on a wet suit, air tank, flippers and mask. They also wear a special jacket full of air, and a belt with weights in it. The diver controls the amount of air in the jacket by pressing a button on an air tube. The air jacket and the weights help the diver to dive down and stay down, and also not to come up again too quickly.

Throwing weights

In some competitions people throw a weight as far as they can. People throw the shot, hammer and discus. Throwing the discus was one of the first Olympic sports in Ancient Greece, more than 2000 years ago. The discus people throw in modern games usually weighs 2 kilograms.

People throw a metal ball called a shot in a sport called shotputting.

GREAT WEIGHTS

Some things are very heavy, other things are light. But when we talk about breaking records with weight we also have to look at relative weight – how heavy something is in relation to something else.

An object that seems heavy to an ant would be incredibly light to a person. And an object that a person struggles to lift might be light as a feather to an elephant.

Ants dragging a grasshopper. Ants can carry 50 times their own weight.

How heavy is a virus?

Viruses are amongst the lightest living things. A virus can weigh as little as 0.0000000000000001 grams! The difference between the weight of a virus and the weight of a person is about the same as the difference between the weight of a person and the weight of the Earth.

Animal weights

The heaviest living insect is the Goliath beetle, which lives in Africa. It can weigh as much as 100 grams. Blue whales are amongst the heaviest living things and can weigh up to 13 800 kilograms. The heaviest dinosaur was the Brachiosaurus, which weighed in at a whopping 81 000 kilograms.

Building blocks

Humans have built with some very weighty building blocks. The average block of stone used to build the Great Pyramid in Egypt weighed about the same as four cars. One of the stones used to build Stonehenge in England weighs about the same as 71 cars. Similar huge building blocks were used in the Inca buildings of Peru and the Aztec pyramids of Mexico. Imagine moving them without any modern lifting equipment! Builders used levers, pulleys and rollers to move the blocks into position.

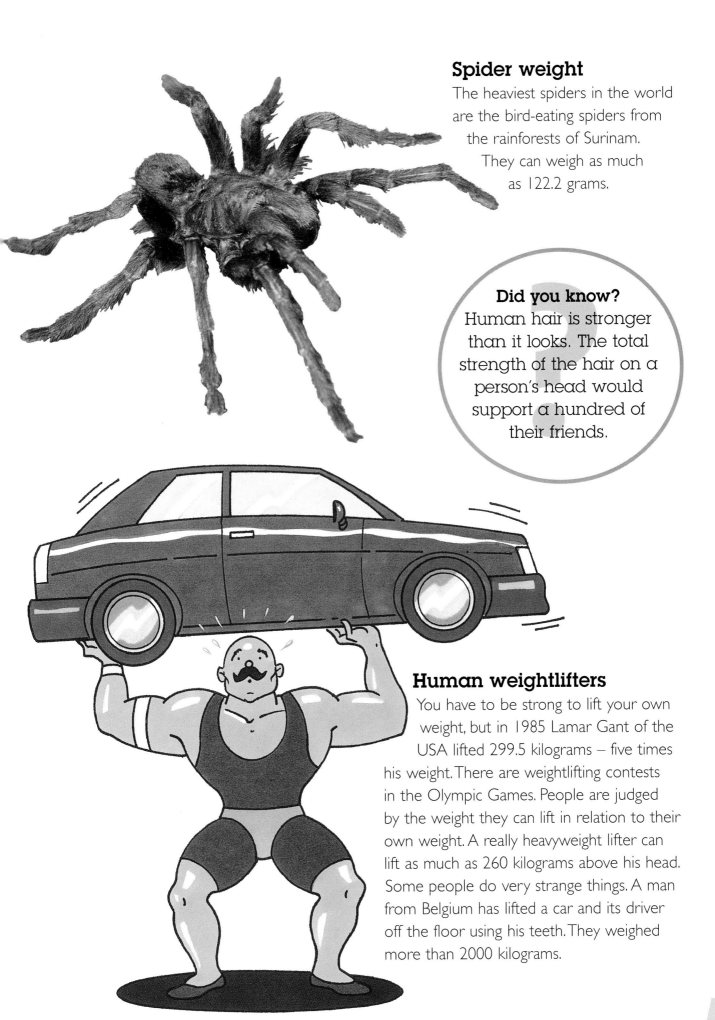

Spider weight
The heaviest spiders in the world are the bird-eating spiders from the rainforests of Surinam. They can weigh as much as 122.2 grams.

Did you know?
Human hair is stronger than it looks. The total strength of the hair on a person's head would support a hundred of their friends.

Human weightlifters
You have to be strong to lift your own weight, but in 1985 Lamar Gant of the USA lifted 299.5 kilograms – five times his weight. There are weightlifting contests in the Olympic Games. People are judged by the weight they can lift in relation to their own weight. A really heavyweight lifter can lift as much as 260 kilograms above his head. Some people do very strange things. A man from Belgium has lifted a car and its driver off the floor using his teeth. They weighed more than 2000 kilograms.

COMPARING WEIGHTS

Now that weights have been standardized all around the world, they can easily be compared with one another. It is useful to be able to compare some common weights and estimate the weight of some everyday items.

Grams and ounces

Light things are measured in grams or ounces. An approximate comparison is that 25 grams is about the same as 1 ounce. In fact 1 ounce is about 28 grams, but 25 is a much easier number to multiply by and goes into 100.

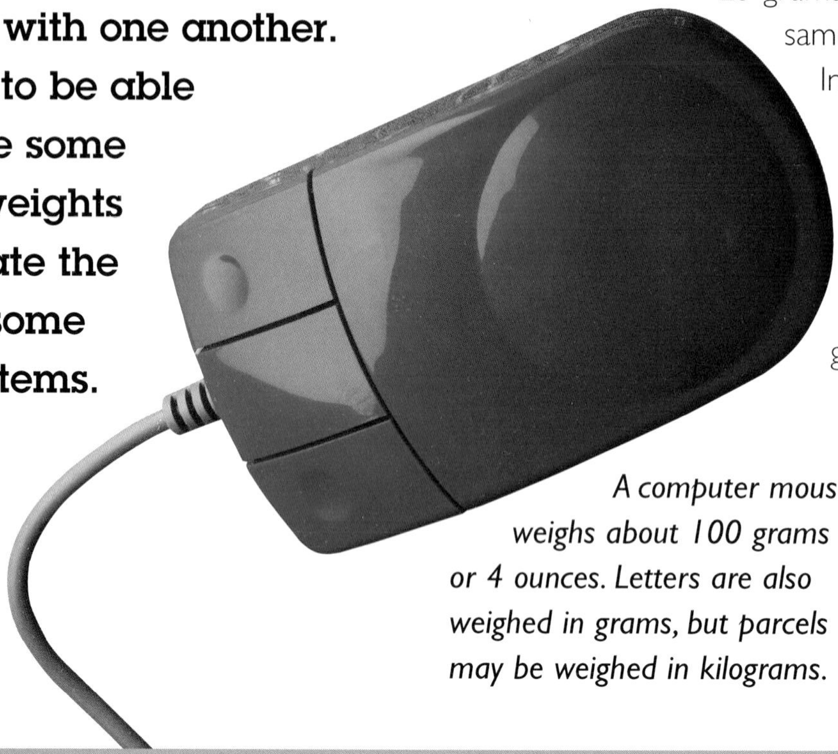

A computer mouse weighs about 100 grams or 4 ounces. Letters are also weighed in grams, but parcels may be weighed in kilograms.

how to change ounces to grams

multiply by 28.3
6 oz = 6x28.3 g
6 oz = 169.8 g

how to change grams to ounces

multiply by 0.04
170 g = 170x0.04 oz
170 g = 6.8 oz

Kilograms and pounds

Heavier objects are weighed in kilograms or pounds. Sometimes the word kilogram is shortened to kilo. There are about 2 ¼ pounds in 1 kilogram.

Fruit and vegetables are usually weighed in pounds or kilograms. A large watermelon can weigh as much as 5 kilograms or about 11 pounds.

An African elephant weighs about 7 tonnes

Tonnes and tons

Very heavy things are weighed in tonnes or tons. A tonne is called a metric ton. There are 1000 kilograms in a tonne, which makes it slightly heavier than a US ton and a little bit lighter than an Imperial ton. Because heavy weights are difficult to estimate, and small differences usually matter less, the three types of ton can be thought of as about the same.

how to change pounds to kilograms

*multiply by 0.45
12 pounds = 12x0.45 kg
12 pounds = 5.4 kg*

how to change kilograms to pounds

*multiply by 2.2
4 kg = 4x2.2 pounds
4 kg = 8.8 pounds*

WEIGHTY WORDS

avoirdupois A system of weighing, still widely used today, that includes ounces, pounds, hundredweights and tons.

carat A measure used to weigh precious stones and metals. One carat weighs 0.2 grams.

counterweight A weight used to make sure the forces on an object are balanced.

dram A unit of weight used by chemists in the past, and sometimes used today.

grain A common unit of weight for hundreds of years, based on the weight of a grain of wheat.

gram (g) A metric unit of weight.

hundredweight (cwt) In imperial units 112 pounds equals 1 hundredweight. In US customary units 100 pounds equals 1 hundredweight.

imperial weights The system of weighing used in Britain before metric weights were introduced. They are based on avoirdupois weights and include ounces, pounds, quarters, stones, hundredweights and tons.

kilogram (kg) A metric unit of weight. There are 1000 grams in 1 kilogram.

kite A weight used in Ancient Egypt.

libra The Roman unit of weight from which the pound weight came. It gave the shortened form of pound (lb).

mass The amount of material in an object. Mass is different to weight because it is not changed by gravity.

metric The most common system of weighing used around the world, always used in science and technology. It is based on units of ten, which makes it part of the decimal system (deci means ten).

microbalance A very accurate machine used to weigh tiny objects.

milligram (mg) A small metric unit of weight. There are 1000 milligrams in 1 gram.

newton (N) In science, the unit used to measure force and weight. (Weight is the force of gravity on mass.)

ounce (oz) A unit of weight used to weigh light objects.

pound (lb) A unit of weight used to weigh heavy objects. There are 16 ounces in an avoirdupois pound.

quarter An imperial and US customary unit of weight. There are 4 quarters in 1 ton.

standard weights Weights that everyone agrees to use. Imperial, US customary and metric weights are all standard units of weight.

stone An imperial unit of weight. There are 14 pounds in 1 stone.

talent An Ancient Greek unit of weight.

ton (t) An imperial and US customary unit of weight used to weigh heavy objects. There are 20 hundredweights in 1 ton. In imperial units this is 2240 pounds (a long ton) and in US customary units it is 2000 pounds (a short ton).

tonne (t) A metric unit of weight used to weigh heavy objects. There are 1000 kilograms in a tonne. The tonne is also called a metric ton.

troy weights Troy weights are used for weighing precious stones and metals. They came from Troyes, in France. There are 12 troy ounces in a troy pound.

unit An agreed amount of something, such as weight, length or volume.

US customary weights The system of weights used in the US, based on the British imperial system. They include ounces, pounds, quarters, hundredweights and tons.

weighbridge A metal plate on a road. It is used for weighing very heavy objects, such as lorries or heavy machinery.

Metric and avoirdupois weights

1 gram = 0.001 kilograms = 0.04 ounces

1 kilogram = 1000 grams = 2.2 pounds

1 metric ton = 1000 kilograms = 2200 pounds

16 drams	= 1 ounce	= 28.3 grams
16 ounces	= 1 pound	= 454 grams
14 pounds	= 1 stone	= 6.35 kilograms
112 pounds	= 1 hundredweight	= 50.8 kilograms
2240 pounds	= 1 (long) ton	= 1016 kilograms
2000 pounds	= 1 (short) ton	= 907 kilograms

INDEX